The Sumerians

NAIDA KIRKPATRICK

Heinemann Library
Chicago, Illinois

© 2003 Heinemann Library
a division of Reed Elsevier Inc.
Chicago, Illinois

Customer Service 888-454-2279

Visit our website at www.heinemannlibrary.com

Map illustrations by John Fleck
Color illustrations by David Westerfield
Photo research by Amor Montes de Oca
Printed and bound in the United States by Lake Book Manufacturing, Inc.

07 06 05 04 03
10 9 8 7 6 5 4 3 2 1

Library of Congress Cataloging-in-Publication Data
Kirkpatrick, Naida.
  The Sumerians / Naida Kirkpatrick.
      v. cm. -- (Understanding people in the past)
Summary: Shows how people lived in ancient Sumeria, a land now known as
Iraq, by describing their social, economic, political, religious, and
cultural life, as well as their contributions to later civilizations.
  ISBN 1-4034-0389-9 (HC), 1-4034-0609-X (Pbk.)
  1. Sumerians--Juvenile literature. [1. Sumerians.] I. Title. II.
Series.
  DS72 .K65 2002
  935'.01--dc21

                            2002002348

Acknowledgments
The author and publisher are grateful to the following for permission to reproduce copyright material:Title page, p.19T The Bridgeman Art Library, New York; p. 5 Werner Forman/Corbis; p. 6 Chris North/Cordaiy Photo Library, Ltd./Corbis; p. 7 Dean Conger/Corbis; p. 8 AFP/Corbis; pp. 9, 11, 12T, 17, 24, 26, 37 The Granger Collection; pp. 10, 12B, 16T, 20, 25T, 27, 29, 41T, 45, 55 Erich Lessing/Art Resource; pp. 13T, 14, 15, 28, 38T, 41B, 46, 47B, 50T, 54T, 57, 59 The Bridgeman Art Library, New York; pp. 13B, 52 North Wind Pictures; pp. 16B, 23, 49 Reunion des Musees Nationaux/Art Resource; p. 18 Art Resource, New York; pp. 19B, 50B Nik Wheeler/Corbis; p. 21 David Lees/Corbis; pp. 22, 30, 43 The British Museum Institution; pp. 25B, 31, 35, 44, 56 Scala/Art Resource; p. 32 Todd Gipstein/Corbis; pp. 33, 39 Bettmann/Corbis; p. 34 Ed Kashi/Corbis; p. 38B Georg Gerster/Photo Researchers, Inc.; p. 42 Winfield I. Parks/National Geographic Image Collection; p. 47T Werner Forman/Art Resource; p. 48 David & Peter Turnley/Corbis; p. 51a Bridgeman Giraudon/Lauros/The Bridgeman Art Library, New York; p. 53 Giraudon/Art Resource; p. 54B Archivo Iconografico, S. A./Corbis

Cover photograph: Erich Lessing/Art Resource

Some words are shown in bold, **like this.** You can find out what they mean by looking in the glossary.

Contents

Who Were the Sumerians?

The Sumerians lived in Sumer from about 3500 B.C.E. until about 2000 B.C.E. The land of Sumer is now part of the country of Iraq. It is hot and dry there. There are no trees and very little stone.

At first, the people lived off the land. They learned to **irrigate** the land and grow crops, as well as raise livestock. They caught fish from the river. Later, they learned to trade with people from other tribes and countries. They traded their farm products and animal skins for metal and wood.

This map shows the location of Sumer and the Tigris and Euphrates Rivers that empty into the Persian Gulf.

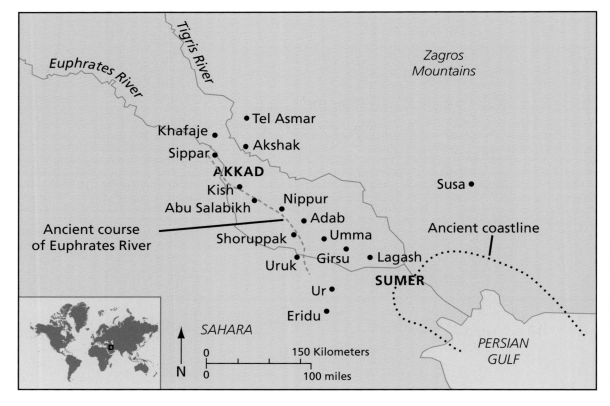

The Sumerians were craftworkers and **artisans.** They used the clay soil to make bricks to build houses and **temples.** They made mats and baskets from the marsh grass. The Sumerians eventually learned to make tools and weapons, as well as cooking utensils and ornaments.

The Sumerians are known for their system of writing. Some of their early records are dated from about 3100 B.C.E. Their writing began as pictures of objects with symbols that showed numbers. Later, the symbols were developed into a written language.

The Sumerians made wooden wheels. These wheels were made in three sections, held together with metal bands. Around the rim were copper studs. The Sumerians also built the first sailboats.

The Sumerians were some of the first people to use sundials, or shadow clocks. They divided the day into twelve parts. Each part was about two hours long. They measured the length of the shadows to tell how much time had passed.

The wheel led to the creation of the chariot. The chariot allowed the Sumerians to be successful in times of war.

The Tigris and Euphrates Rivers

When the ancestors of the ancient Sumerians arrived in the Tigris and Euphrates River Valley, they found a hot, dry land. The wind stirred up a powdery, choking dust. In the winter, the south wind brought rains that turned everything to mud. In the spring, everything became green. The melting snows in the Zagros and other mountains to the north drained into the Tigris and Euphrates Rivers. Sometimes this caused flooding. Over time, this flooding caused the build up of dirt **levees,** or embankments. This made it easier to drain the fields and raise crops. There were fish and waterfowl in the nearby swamps and marshes. These were caught by the Sumerians and eaten.

Several cities grew along the Tigris and Euphrates Rivers. This area became known as Mesopotamia, which means "the land between two rivers."

The Persian Gulf, along with the Tigris and Euphrates Rivers, helped the Sumerians remain in contact with each other and their neighbors.

Sumer stretched from the present-day city of Baghdad (Iraq) to the Persian Gulf. There are no trees and little stone here. Wood was often used to build fires for cooking and heating, and stone was often used for building. But the Sumerians had to use something else. They used the soil to make clay, or mud, bricks to build their homes.

The Sumerians learned to dig canals and **reservoirs** to hold the water when the rivers flooded. This water was used for the crops during the dry season. Everyone in the village helped build the canals so they would have enough water throughout the year. The villages along the rivers grew to become cities. The rivers were used for travel and trade.

How Do We Know About the Sumerians?

Mounds and artifacts

Archaeologists help uncover the history of ancient peoples, including the Sumerians. Because many Sumerian buildings were made of mud brick, they did not last. Rain and floods buried everything. Nothing was left except mounds.

In the 1800s, archaeologists examined many of these mounds in the desert of Iraq. They wanted to learn about these ancient cities. They discovered Sumerian **temples** dating from about 3000 B.C.E. They found hundreds of clay **tablets** with writing on them.

Artifacts were found at burial sites. These

These workmen are helping to excavate a Sumerian home. Their work helps us to learn about how Sumerian cities were built.

help us learn about the customs of ancient people. The Sumerians left many artifacts of gold, silver, and **lapis lazuli** in tombs.

Archaeologists found statues of Gudea in the area that was once Sumer. Gudea was a ruler of the city of Lagash. In about 2200 B.C.E., Lagash was under the control of the Gutians. Gudea was a successful trader as well as a prince. He became powerful enough to be made a ruler of Lagash. He brought fair government to his people. Gudea preserved the Sumerian culture through his writings and by building temples. He used much gold, silver, and semi-precious stones in these temples.

Known as "the seated scribe," this statue of Gudea is from about 2150 B.C.E. The lower part is inscribed with **cuneiform** symbols that praise his deeds and wish him a long life.

Paintings and writing
Archaeologists also discovered Sumerian art such as wall paintings and copper statues. Two large cylinders were found among artifacts at Lagash. They were **inscribed** by Gudea with 1,400 lines of writing. This is the longest example of Sumerian writing.

Another way of learning about ancient people is from their writings on clay tablets and on statues. The people who study these writings are called **epigraphists**.

History in Pictures and Words

The Sumerians used a form of writing that we call **cuneiform.** They made lists of the number of cattle, bags of grain, or sales of land. Sometimes messages were **inscribed,** or carved, on an upright stone called a **stele.** One famous limestone stele is from 2425 B.C.E. It shows King Eannatum of Lagash leading his army into battle on one side. On the other side is a huge god, Ningirsu, holding a net that contains the defeated army. Stele were also often used as boundary markers.

The Sumerians made figures of priests or rulers with round, staring eyes made of shell and black limestone. Some were found in **temples.** They may have been put there to offer prayers.

The Standard of Ur
Life in ancient Sumer is shown in a detailed wooden object known as the Standard of Ur. The Standard of Ur consists of two, eighteen-inch-wide panels. They are inlaid with shell and **lapis lazuli.** One side shows soldiers in battle and leading prisoners to the king. The opposite side shows the king at a banquet. The people of the village are bringing gifts of livestock, produce, and goods. These were the basis of Sumerian wealth because they were used in trade.

This is an inscription of the *Epic of Gilgamesh* on a clay **tablet.**

Gilgamesh

The most famous Sumerian poem is the *Epic of Gilgamesh.* An epic is a long poem telling about the deeds of a hero. The poem describes the battles fought and won by Gilgamesh, a king who ruled Uruk in about 2700 B.C.E. Later, when the Babylonians conquered Sumer, they added more to the stories of Gilgamesh.

Writing

Sumerian writing is thought to be the first written language. More than 1,000 small clay **tablets inscribed** with **script** were found in Mesopotamia. These date from about 3100 B.C.E. Most were lists of supplies of grain and numbers of cattle. Some of these were small tags that were attached to sacks of grain like a shipping tag. Large tablets had columns of marks to keep accounts.

This is an accounting tablet with **cuneiform** writing. It shows a record of loaves of bread and barley cakes.

Archaeologists found many statues, stones, and vases inscribed with the names of different people. In about 2500 B.C.E., contracts of land sales began to appear. These were found in the remains of houses.

In 2100 B.C.E., Sumerian schools became important centers of learning. Many thousands of documents have been uncovered. One of these was the earliest known written code of law.

How did they write?

A pointed reed stylus, or pen, was used to make marks on a damp clay tablet. Eventually, they stopped using the pointed reed stylus. Scribes probably found it left messy ridges in the clay. They chose the

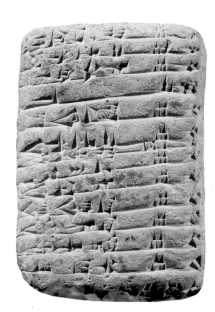

This tablet lists barley rations for seventeen gardeners for one month.

triangular shaped stylus. This could be pushed down into the soft clay and was not messy.

Writing records

At first, writing was used to record sacks of grain. The symbols were written in vertical columns, beginning at the top right-hand corner of each tablet. By 3000 B.C.E., Sumerian **scribes** decided it was better to turn the tablets and write in horizontal lines. This made the writing quicker and they avoided smudging the words or numbers as they wrote.

Sumerian scribes carried out the work of keeping records. Other people may have written, too, but we do not know what they wrote.

We don't know whether Sumerian scribes had a special name for their writing. Today, we know it as cuneiform.

Here is a **bas-relief** sculpture showing two scribes taking notes.

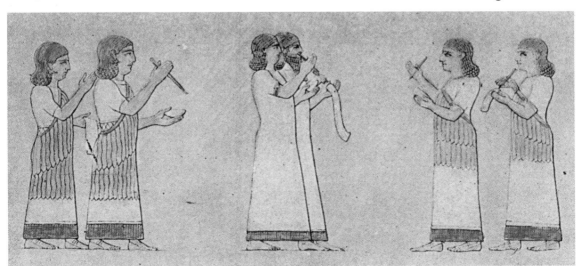

Building a Civilization

5000–3500 B.C.E.

The world's first civilization began in Sumer and the first people to settle there were the Abaidians. Their settlements eventually became the first Sumerian cities. These cities were: Adab, Eridu, Isin, Kish, Kullab, Lagash, Larsa, Nippur, and Ur.

3400–2900 B.C.E.

By about 3250 B.C.E., people migrated to the area from the northeast, possibly from central Asia. It is not certain who they were. They spoke a different language and called themselves "the black-headed ones," possibly because of their black hair.

This baked clay prism lists all the Sumerian kings in **cuneiform script.**

There were many kings in the **city-states** of Sumer. The first ruler of Sumer was Etanna of Kish. He ruled around 3000 B.C.E. His deeds were recorded by poets and storytellers.

2112–2004 B.C.E.

The Dynasty of Ur was founded by Ur-Nammu. Ur-Nammu named himself the "King of Sumer and Akkad." He won a battle against the King of Lagash. He also built **irrigation** works that helped the farmers. He built docks along the river for trade.

Ur-Nammu wrote a code of laws. He made the laws to ensure there was justice for his people. He also created a system of honest weights and measures.

The next king was Shulgi. He was a warrior, too. He gave himself the title, "King of the Four Quarters." Under his rule, trade prospered as well as literature and the schools for **scribes.**

During this time, the **ziggurat** was first created. A ziggurat is a layered tower with a **shrine** at the top. It was used for religious worship.

This ziggurat was built in the city of Ur to honor the moon god, Nanna.

Government

City-states

Around 4000–3500 B.C.E., the villages and towns of Sumer became **city-states.** City-states were made up of the ruling god, king, royalty, priests, craftworkers, farmers, **merchants,** slaves, and free citizens. The people had great respect for law and justice. The Sumerians were the first people to make laws protecting each person's rights. They did not want these rights taken away.

This is the Code of Hammurabi from 1790 B.C.E. There are 282 laws listed on it.

Rulers

The responsibilities of the king were to build **temples,** maintain the canals that **irrigated** the farmland, and make sure the laws were followed. He also built an army. The army used chariots and had soldiers who wore heavy armor.

The first rulers of Sumer were common men who were elected by a group of the city's free citizens. The Sumerians believed that each city had a special god that looked after the people. The king chosen by the people also had to be approved by the god. After about 3000 B.C.E., the position of ruler was handed down from father to son.

Attendants, like the one shown here, might have helped kings with various matters.

A group of free adult citizens met on an **ad hoc** basis to make decisions for the city. This group was called upon to decide punishment. They also made decisions about large-scale projects such as canal digging, or what should be done during the threat of war. These decisions were taken to the king, who then made his own ruling.

Record-keeping and laws

As early as 2500 B.C.E., some merchants and traders began to make records of their business transactions on clay **tablets.** As the cities grew, it was necessary to buy land and slaves to carry out the work on the farms and in the city. This made it necessary to keep good records. There were legal records made of sales of property, fields, and slaves.

The earliest known written code of laws is that of Ur-Nammu, king of the Sumerian city of Ur in about 2100 B.C.E. Some of these laws were about arguments between two people. Some gave justice to the poor. Others maintained honest trade in the marketplace by regulating the system of weights and measures.

This Sumerian law tablet dates from around 1868–57 B.C.E. Its **cuneiform** writing shows about 40 of the oldest documented laws in history. These laws refer to land, slavery, inheritance, and marriage.

Uruk

Uruk was the **city-state** where An, the heaven god, lived. It was one of the capitals of Sumer. At one time, the ruler of Uruk was King Gilgamesh, the hero from the *Epic of Gilgamesh.*

The Mosaic **Temple** at Uruk is dedicated to An and dates from 3000 B.C.E. Most temples were built on platforms so that they were much taller than the surrounding buildings. The temple was a link between the gods in heaven and the people on Earth.

The temple at Uruk was built on a 40-foot (12-meter) high artificial hill. A stairway leads to a small **whitewashed shrine** at the top. The architects of Uruk shaped small cones of

These are the remains of the Mosaic Temple at Uruk. It shows the round ends of the cones. Architects made triangles, zigzags, and other designs with colored cones.

Many seals were found in Uruk. Seals were often used as signatures and were pressed into clay.

clay and dipped them in different colors of paint. They stuck these cones into the thick mud plaster covering the temple's walls and columns.

Lugalzaggesi was the last king of Uruk. He called himself "King of Uruk and King of the Land." He believed that he brought peace, happiness, and prosperity to the land. Lugalzaggesi was king for about twenty years until Uruk was conquered by Sargon the Great.

Sargon joined Sumer and the northern half of Mesopotamia into a single nation. Sargon's empire lasted for almost 200 years. The next conquerors of Sargon's empire were the Gutians. They came from the mountains of the east in 2200 B.C.E. They ruled for 100 years before they were overthrown by Utehegal of Uruk, who became King of Sumer.

The ruins of Uruk are still visible today. Here a man and child stand in the ruins of the ancient city in modern-day Iraq.

Around 4000 B.C.E., the Ubaidians built one of the first Sumerian settlements. It was called Ur. By 2800 B.C.E., it was a prosperous Sumerian **city-state.** Ur was built on the Euphrates River. This location was ideal for business because grain and goods could be moved along the river to other cities.

A large **tablet** describing work done by craftworkers was found in Ur. It dates from around 1975 B.C.E. It tells of the work of the sculptor, the jeweler, the stone worker, the carpenter, leatherworker, and basketmaker. It also tells how the work was done. This work was important because many of the things made were traded with other countries.

There is not much known about the Second Dynasty of Ur, because so far there have been no records found for this period.

The Third Dynasty was around 2050 B.C.E. The **ziggurat** was the most important building of the city. It was built on a high terrace in the center of the city. It held many **shrines,** storehouses, **magazines,** and homes for people who worked in the **temple.** The temples in the large cities were very big.

This statue discovered in a grave at Ur symbolized fertility and may have been used in religious ceremonies. It is made of wood and covered with gold. The coat is made of shell, and the horns and eyes of **lapis lazuli**. It is called "Ram Caught in a Thicket."

Much of Ur still remains, like the ziggurat and walls seen here.

They were almost like a city themselves. Temples were a sign of wealth and power.

The destruction of a Sumerian temple was the worst event that could happen to a city and its people. The people believed their purpose in life was to serve their gods. All directions and instructions came from the gods.

In 2000 B.C.E. warriors from Elam, a country to the east of Sumer, attacked Ur and carried off the king. This story was told in the *Lamentation over the Destruction of Ur.* A lamentation is a poem about the misfortune and defeat of a city. Lamentations have been found on clay tablets.

A riddle from Ur
On a tablet excavated at Ur, **archaeologists** found this riddle. Can you guess the answer?

A house which like heaven has a plan, Which like a copper kettle is cloth covered, Which like a goose stands on a base, He whose eyes are not open enters it, He whose eyes are (wide) open comes out of it.

Answer: It is a school!

Family Life

There is a Sumerian proverb that says, "Friendship lasts a day; kinship lasts forever." This proverb is repeated in many of the legends and stories of Sumer.

Marriage contracts between two families would have been written on **tablets** like this.

Marriage

Family was important to the Sumerians. Parents loved and cared for their children. Children loved their parents and obeyed them. When a young man was old enough to marry, his parents made arrangements with the parents of a young woman. As soon as the young man gave a bridal gift to the father of the girl, the engagement was official. When this was done, a contract was written on a clay tablet. We do not know how old the bride and groom typically were.

In Sumer, a woman could own property and have a business. She could also serve as a witness in cases of disagreement.

Children

Children were under the authority of their parents. If the parents chose, they could sell them into slavery. Sometimes if a man owed many debts, he would sell himself and his family into slavery for a period of about

The Sumerians wrote many poems. Often, poems were meant to be accompanied by a musical instrument, such as a **lyre.**

three years. Children whose parents died were often adopted.

There were many long poems written about love and special people or gods. One is written about Dumuzi and the goddess Inanna. It is a long poem with many verses.

Sumerian Clothing

We learn how the Sumerians dressed from looking at statues and carvings on bowls and vases.

Men

Some men had long beards. They usually had long hair parted down the middle. They wore a woven wool skirt. Over this, a garment like a shawl was worn over the left shoulder, leaving the right arm bare. Sometimes men wore a long, felt cloak. Men probably wore sandals. Some images of Sumerian soldiers show them wearing boots.

Women

Women wore dresses that looked like long shawls. Their left shoulder was covered, leaving their right arm bare. Women also had long hair which was usually parted down the middle and braided. Women often wore coverings on their heads. These coverings were made of linen, ribbons, and beads. Women also probably wore leather sandals.

Children

We do not know how children dressed. It is possible that their clothing was the same as their parents.

These statues show how some Sumerian men dressed.

Cloth and skins

Goats, sheep, and lambs were raised by the Sumerians for their wool. A spindle was used to spin the wool, which was then woven into cloth. Spinning and weaving was done by three women. It took as many as eight days to make a piece of cloth about 3.5 x 4 yards (3 x 3.6 meters). Flax was grown and its fibers were woven to make linen cloth.

The cloth was then taken to the fullers. A fuller is a person who soaks cloth in a special solution in a large vat. He stomped on the cloth as it was soaking. This was probably done to condition the fabric.

Skins from bulls, calves, pigs, and sheep were tanned. The skins were then rubbed with fats and oils to make them soft. Leather was used to make sandals, harnesses, saddles, and special bags to hold water.

Jewelry

The Sumerians wore jewelry. The women wore beads and pendants in their headdresses. They wore rings made of ivory and gold or silver. Some of the wealthy had jewelry with stones such as **lapis lazuli,** carnelian, and topaz.

Women dressed similarly to men in that they wore long skirts with the same type of looped fabric. The woman below is wearing a headdress that covers all her hair.

Growing Up and Going to School

The Sumerians established some of the first schools. The Sumerian school was called "edubba" or "**tablet** house." At first, schools were used mainly to train **scribes.** Later, the Sumerians developed several other areas of study including religion, zoology, geography, mathematics, grammar, language, and geology.

Girls

Girls did not go to school. They remained at home, where they learned to cook, make cloth, and take care of the family. If they were from a wealthy family, they might have learned to play musical instruments. There were special schools where musicians were taught. There is no evidence that women were scribes.

The poor

Most students came from wealthy families. The poor could not afford to send a son to school. He was needed to work on his family's farm or to work in his father's shop.

Scribe school

The head of the school was called "Ummia," which means "expert" or "school father." A student was called "school son." The teacher was called "big brother." "Big brother's" duty was to prepare work for the student, examine

> **Sexagesimal**
> The Sumerians developed a number system called **sexagesimal.** It was based on the number 60. We still use some of this system when we divide a circle into 60 degrees or an hour into 60 minutes.

This clay figurine of a wheeled animal might have been a child's toy.

the student's writing, and hear him recite his studies from memory. Other teachers were known as "the man in charge of drawing," "the man in charge of Sumerian," and "the man in charge of the whip." The whip was often used to encourage the student to work harder. It was also used to maintain order in the classroom.

Scribe schools were not easy. The student scribe attended school from childhood until graduating as a young man. The school day was long and students were punished often in order to make them pay attention. When a young scribe graduated, he was in great demand by **merchants,** royalty, or anyone who needed something written down. Scribes did important work like managing estates and surveying land. They acted as judges and settled arguments and claims.

Language was the most important school subject. The Sumerians traded with many other people who spoke different languages, so scribes needed to be able to understand them. Students memorized lists containing hundreds of **cuneiform** words and phrases, both in Sumerian and Akkadian.

This is a statuette of a schoolmaster from Lagash, known as "Dudu, the Scribe." There were thousands of scribes, including junior, high, royal, and **temple** scribes. Some scribes became leading government officials.

A typical school day
School started at sunrise. Students studied tablets prepared the day before, then they were given a new tablet prepared by the "big brother." They studied and copied the new tablet. Later, it was examined by "big brother" and "school father" to see whether it was copied accurately. Most lessons were memorized.

What Did the Sumerians Believe?

The Sumerians believed in many gods. They believed that when the earth was created, the gods divided the land between themselves. The gods created the *me* (pronounced may). The *me* was a set of laws to keep the world in order.

The Sumerians believed the god, Enki, created humans. The myths and poems of Sumer tell that the gods were having difficulty getting food. Enki created a man from the clay and gave him the image of the gods. The Sumerians believed that humans were supposed to serve the gods. They were to give them food, drink, and a place to live. The gods were then free to carry out their divine duties.

Death

The Sumerians believed that when a person died, their spirit went to another world and did not return. They called this place the **netherworld.** They built tombs and buried the dead with their personal belongings to take on their journey to the netherworld. Many Sumerian myths, songs, and poems were written about this custom.

This statuette shows a man in worship. Often, Sumerians would place statuettes like this one in **temples** to "pray" for them when they could not.

The Sumerians believed that the gods controlled their crops. They saw the brown meadows as a time when the gods died. When the fields bloomed again, celebrations were held to celebrate the resurrection of the gods.

Sin was believed to be inborn. When a person suffered, it was the work of the gods. The best way to end the suffering was to glorify the gods and wait for them to end the pain.

The Sumerians had many heroes, both real and imaginary. One famous hero was King Gilgamesh. Stories about him were written in the long poem called *The Epic of Gilgamesh.*

Utu was the Sumerian god of the sun. Many statues were made in his image.

Sumerian gods

There were four leading **deities.** They were known as the creating gods. They were the four major parts of the universe:

•An, god of heaven
•Ki, goddess of earth
•Enlil, god of air
•Enki, god of water

Next in importance were these gods:

•Nanna, god of the moon
•Utu, god of the sun
•Inanna, goddess of love and war
•Ninurta, god of the violent and destructive south wind

Ceremonies and Temples

Temples

The Sumerians believed each city had a special god who protected them. In the cities, the people built a special **temple** as a home for their **deity.** Temples grew to become elaborate structures set on top of a high mud brick platform. These early temples developed into the temple tower or **ziggurat.**

Sumerian temples had two special features. There was a niche, a hollowed-out place in a wall, for a statue of the god. In front of the statue was an **offering** table made of mud brick.

The temple was a holy place that needed to be cared for every day. There were officials, workers, and slaves to take care of the temple. Many **scribes** worked at the temple. Musicians and singers performed in some of the religious services.

Offerings

Daily offerings were made by the priests. These offerings included food, water, wine, beer, spices, and incense. Hymns and prayers were written for temple services. Music was important in the temple as well as other

This statue was found in a Sumerian temple. The Sumerians believed constant prayer was important to the well-being of each person. Since it was not practical to pray constantly, a statue was made to place before the altar as a substitute for the individual.

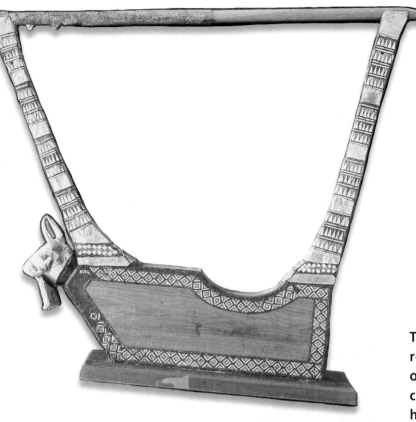

This **lyre** was reconstructed from one found at the royal cemetery at Ur. It may have been used in temple ceremonies.

places. Many hymns to the gods have been uncovered on **tablets** that were probably used in the temple.

Lamentations

When a city was destroyed, a lamentation was written. A lamentation is a long poem telling of the destruction of the city and the troubles of its people. *The Lamentation over Ur*, and *The Lamentation over Nippur,* tell of such terrible events.

Medicine and Healing

A medical doctor in Sumer was known as *a-zu*.
A **tablet excavated** at Ur from about 2700 B.C.E.
bears the **inscription**, "Lulu, the Doctor." Sumerians
believed demons caused their sickness. They would
have gone to someone like Lulu for help.

Ancient prescriptions

One Sumerian doctor made a list of his favorite
prescriptions on a tablet. Fifteen ancient Sumerian
prescriptions have been found by **archaeologists** in
this way. These prescriptions help us to see how the
Sumerians treated illness and injury.

This tablet describes
in **cuneiform** how to
"pulverize [crush] pears
and the roots of manna
plant then put this in
beer and let the sick
man drink."

Fennel, an herb, was sometimes chewed or drunk with water to cure a stomachache. Medicines were made from other plants such as myrtle—a type of shrub—and the herb thyme. Trees such as willow, pear, fir, and date were also used for medicine. Medicine was made from the seeds, roots, branches, bark, or sap of trees. These were either solid or ground into a powder. Sumerian doctors also used milk, snakeskin, and turtle shell in their medicines.

Doctors made salves of powder mixed with "kushumma" wine and cedar tree oil. Some powders were dissolved in beer or milk and drunk. These treatments were probably given to bring down a fever, relieve stomach pain, or sooth a cough.

Sometimes, prescriptions called for the ingredients to be ground into a powder and mixed with a liquid to make a paste. The paste was then placed over the sick part of the body as a **poultice.** A poultice may have been made of "rotten grain" and placed on a wound. The fungi in the spoiled grain probably produced an antibiotic that helped the wound to heal.

This Sumerian tablet contains the world's oldest-known medical handbook. Part of the right-hand column reads: "White pear tree, the flower of the 'moon' plant, grind into a powder, dissolve in beer, let the man drink."

The Farming Year

Archaeologists excavated a site called Jarmo in the foothills of the Zagros Mountains. They discovered mud houses. The houses had ovens with chimneys and **hearths.** The archaeologists determined that this farming settlement was from about 7000 B.C.E. They found stone axes with polished cutting edges, stone spindle **whorls** for weaving, and stone cups and bowls.

Archaeologists found tools such as **mortars** and **pestles** for grinding grain, and sickle blades made of flint. In other areas, stone hoes and grinding stones were found.

In Sumer, farmers plowed and planted seed at the same time. Sumerian farmers grew barley,

This grain is being harvested using methods that were used by the ancient Sumerians.

peas, beans, and two kinds of wheat. They also grew onions, garlic, lettuce, turnips, chickpeas, lentils, leeks, mustard, and cucumbers. Many of these vegetables are still grown in the area today.

Cows were an important part of the Sumerian diet. They raised cows for their milk and often depicted farming scenes like this in **temples.**

A set of instructions was written to help farmers. These instructions were called a *Farmers Almanac.* An almanac has information about growing crops and the best ways and times to plant.

Animals were important to the Sumerians. Goats and sheep were raised for their wool. Goats and cows were raised for their milk. Cattle and pigs were raised for their meat. Donkeys were used mostly for transportation. Animal skins were often tanned into leather.

The Sumerians were skillful engineers. They built a system of canals, dikes, and **reservoirs** in order to make the best use of the water supply for farming.

A Sumerian City

At the center of a Sumerian city stood the **temple.** This was where the chief **deity** of the city lived. Sometimes smaller temples were built nearby for the relatives of the deity.

Houses

Most Sumerian homes were one or two stories, but there were a few that were three stories tall. Cities did not seem to be built according to any plan. Large houses were built next to small ones.

Streets

Many streets were narrow and winding. Streets were probably not paved. Some streets were narrow alleys that led only to

This illustration of a Sumerian city shows the walls around the city, and the walls around the temple compound.

This picture shows what remains today of the living and business areas of the city of Ur.

houses hidden away in the middle of a large block of buildings. In the center of a city, possibly near the temple, was a public square. Leading to this square were wide streets where people could walk and visit with friends. Feasts and other events were held in the public square.

Taking out the trash

Cities had no system for disposing of garbage and waste. It was simply thrown out onto the street. After a time, it piled up until it rose above the level of the doorstep. There is no record about what the Sumerians did when this happened.

Defensive walls

Cities were surrounded with walls with massive gates. These were built for defense. It is possible that the walls were also meant to protect people against harsh weather.

Architects and Builders

Early houses dating to about 3500 B.C.E. were huts made of flimsy reed and mud. Gradually, Sumerians began to build their houses of mud brick, because there was not much stone available. Several types of brick were used. The most common was a rectangular brick made of mud with a straw binder. Straw was added to the mud to keep the brick from breaking apart. Sometimes square or loaf-shaped bricks were used.

The Sumerians often used loaf-shaped bricks when building. Here is a pattern created by the bricks used in this wall.

The earliest **temples** were only simple **shrines** with a crude altar and table for **offerings.** As the villages grew, the temples were made larger. They became elaborate structures set on top of mud brick platforms. The foundations were usually made of rough blocks of limestone.

In 3200 B.C.E., the White Temple was built in Uruk and dedicated to the sky god, An. It was called the White Temple because the long, narrow inner shrine was **whitewashed.**

38

This is part of the **Stele** of Ur-Nammu. Ur-Nammu founded the third dynasty of Ur. During his seventeen-year reign, he built and restored temples in Ur, as well as in other cities of Sumer.

By about 3000 B.C.E., a new type of brick was made. It was called the plano-convex brick. It was flat on one side and curved on the other side. Now it was possible to make an oval shaped building with curved walls. Some of the buildings at Uruk were decorated with colorful cones set into the walls to make designs.

The ancient city of Babylon, near Sumer, was surrounded by massive walls. The walls were the city's main security against attack. Over many years, the walls were damaged during wars. Many different kings worked to rebuild the walls. The part of the wall along the Euphrates River was built right down to the waterline. The wall also served as a breakwater to protect the city from floods.

A Sumerian Home

The average Sumerian house was made up of several rooms. The outside walls were often six feet (about two meters) thick to keep the house cool. Rooms were arranged around an open courtyard. There were no windows. Most average houses were only one story. There were rooms for sleeping and there was a kitchen.

Wealthier Sumerians lived in two story houses that had about twelve rooms. Houses were made of plastered brick, **whitewashed** inside and out. Whitewash is a thin mixture of lime and water. White color is added and this mixture is used to paint walls.

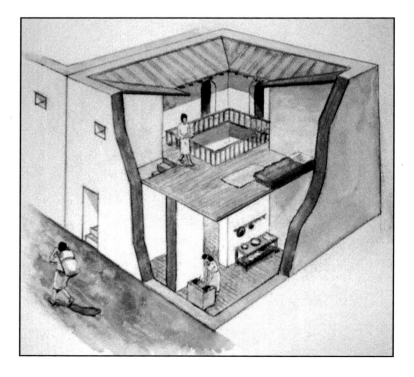

This drawing of a two-story townhouse from Ur shows rooms arranged around a central courtyard. All the rooms on the first level opened onto the courtyard. On the second level the rooms opened onto a gallery.

The ground floor had a reception room, a kitchen with a fireplace and clay, stone, and copper utensils. There was also a toilet, servants quarters, and a workroom or storeroom on the first floor. Sometimes there was a room for guests, as well as a private chapel. The doors of the first floor rooms opened onto a brick paved courtyard. There was a drain in the center of the courtyard to carry away rainwater. The courtyard also permitted light into the windowless rooms.

This bull head may have been a mount for a piece of furniture or for a harp.

Stairs led to the second-story gallery. This was made of wood and was about three feet (one meter) wide, supported by wooden poles. The doors of the family living quarters opened onto the gallery.

The roof was flat or slightly sloped and was reached by a ladder. Families often slept on the roof because it was much cooler there. Under the house, there was a special place where dead family members were buried. There were some special cemeteries for the dead outside the cities, but we do not know why everyone was not buried there.

Sumerian families had beds, couches, chairs, and tables in their homes. This sculpture shows a woman sleeping on a bed.

Cooking and Eating

Each Sumerian home had a kitchen for preparing food for the family. They ate many different vegetables, grains, and meats. Sumerians used barley, wheat, and millet for bread and cakes. Barley kernels could be beaten into coarse pieces and cooked as a kind of **porridge.** It was also ground into flour and baked into flat bread. The flat bread and cakes were probably baked in an oven or on a hot, flat stone. This type of bread is still eaten in the region today.

The Sumerians made stews using small pieces of meat and different vegetables. Sesame oil was possibly used for cooking. Sometimes beer was added to other food to add flavor. They may have used honey to sweeten some foods, too.

These present-day fishermen, using a narrow curved boat in the shallow marsh, have caught a fish with a spear. This technique is much like that of the ancient Sumerians.

This gold bowl was found inside a tomb. **Archaeologists** found a silver tube inside the bowl, indicating that it was probably a drinking cup and the tube was a straw.

Meat

A special butcher was in charge of preparing meat. The Sumerians liked pork. They also ate deer, wild boar, gazelles, and birds. They caught fish by spearing them and by using nets.

Eating in the city

People who lived in the cities got their food from the **bazaar**. There, a variety of vegetables and fruits, as well as cheese, spices, dried fish, mutton, pork, and duck were available.

Preserving food

The Sumerians needed to preserve food for use when there were no crops. They dried meat and fish as well as dates, figs, and other fruits.

Kash

The favorite drink of the Sumerians was beer. It was called "kash." Kash was a thick beer, almost like porridge. The Sumerians used reeds or metal straws to drink their beer.

Feasts and Fun

The Sumerians celebrated special holidays. Some months had special names such as "The Month of the Eating of the Gazelles," or "The Month of the Feast of Shulgi." Some months were named for the gods of a specific city, and thus were different in each city.

The most important holiday was the New Year. This was the celebration of the holy marriage between Dumuzi and the goddess Inanna. The celebrations lasted for several days. There were other feasts on the day of the new moon, the 7th, 15th, and the last day of the month.

Summer and winter

Dumuzi was married to the goddess Inanna. When Inanna felt her husband did not love her, she sent him to the underworld for six months. This caused the hot, dry summer when nothing grew. At the beginning of the Sumerian New Year, Dumuzi returned to Earth. The reunion between Dumuzi and Inanna caused everything to grow again.

The top section of this **stele** shows a feast. A man and woman with servants, a harpist, and dancers are all present.

Music

Musicians performed in the **temple,** but they also performed in the public square for everyone. Some of the instruments that have been **excavated** include drums, tambourines, and reed and metal pipes. Other instruments used by musicians were several types of **lyres** and harps. People probably danced to some of this music.

Other fun activities were held in the public square. Some of the events were wrestling matches, gambling, and storytelling. There was also a tavern for the older citizens.

This board game was found in the royal tomb of Ur. **Archaeologists** believe it to be the oldest board game.

Crafts and Trades

The **ziggurat** was a **temple** where the **deity** of the city lived, but it was used for other purposes, too. There were places at the ziggurat for the workshops of many Sumerian craftworkers.

Metalsmiths used copper and tin to make bronze. Some craftworkers knew how to spin gold and silver into threads for **filigree.** They also beat gold and silver into thin sheets, then hammered the sheets over wood. This was made into jewelry and statues.

Wool from sheep was spun into thread and woven on looms to make fabric and felt. Goat hair was used to make carpets. Those skilled in **lapidary** arts made jewelry, such as rings, bracelets, and pendants, from precious stones and pearls.

These pieces of jewelry were found in the tomb of Queen Puabi, at Ur. They show the artistic accomplishments of the jewelers. They date from about 2600 B.C.E.

By 3500 B.C.E., the potters wheel began to be used. Potters learned to operate a kiln and fire the clay. Sometimes their work was decorated.

Around 3000 B.C.E., bricks made of clay were baked either in the sun or in an oven. They were used to line wells and construct arches. The soft clay was used as **tablets.**

Queen Puabi wore an elaborate headdress, and many strings of beads. She had rings on all her fingers. Only a wealthy person could dress this way.

By 2500 B.C.E., the Sumerians began to make glass. No one knows how glassmaking got started in the area. It is possible that craftworkers accidentally created glass when experimenting with sand, quartz, soda, and lime.

Carpenters made furniture and ships. Their tools included hammers, chisels, saws, and drills. Basket makers used marsh reeds to make woven containers. They also built fences and huts.

Gold was first beaten into thin sheets before a craftworker could shape it into a helmet.

Sumerian Merchants and Traders

Merchants

Traveling **merchants** and traders kept cities in contact with each other and with other parts of the ancient world. Merchants created the **bazaar. Artisans** and craftworkers sold their handmade items. They were paid in kind, which means they exchanged their goods for other goods. They did not have coin money. Usually a silver disk or ring of a standard weight was given in payment.

Traders

Some traders were more adventurous. They led their donkey caravans across the Syrian Desert, to the Mediterranean coast. Traders also sailed across the Persian Gulf to India. They traded with Somaliland and Ethiopia in Africa.

This present-day bazaar in the Middle East shows the variety of goods that can be found. At Sumerian bazaars, people could buy pots, clothing, and other local products. They could also buy imported items such as ivory combs from India or beads from Iran.

Traders exchanged grain, wool, and cloth for cedar and cypress wood. They often brought back gold, silver, ivory, pearls, shells, and semi-precious stones. Another trade item was obsidian from eastern Turkey. It was used to make tools.

Sumerian craftworkers made tools, weapons, and jewelry from these supplies. Some goods they used themselves, and other goods they traded back for more raw materials.

Traders returned to Sumeria with tales of foreign people with different languages and beliefs. These stories were found on **tablets.**

These tokens were used in trade. Since there was no money, a stone of a certain value was used to determine the amount of sale. These tokens were **excavated** in Uruk.

Transportation and Trade

The wheel

In about 4000 B.C.E., the Sumerians built the first known vehicle with wheels. It was probably a chariot, but the wheel could be used on many kinds of carts.

The wheel was made of three pieces of wood, fastened together with metal bands. Copper studs were placed on the edge of the wheel to keep the wheel from slipping. The solid wooden wheel was used for centuries without being changed.

Animals

The animal most commonly used for transportation was the donkey. Toward the end of the Sumerian civilization, horses were known, but not used much. The ox was used to pull carts, **sledges,** and plows.

The common boat in use during Sumerian times is still used today in Iraq. It is called the *guffa*, but in ancient times it was known as "the turnip." It was made of reeds, covered with skin and shaped like a basket.

The Sumerians used rowboats for travel on the water. Oars were used to move the boat. Rowboats were used to ferry grain and textiles to other cities along the river.

Boats and ships

It was easy to guide rowboats downriver, but going upstream against the current was difficult. Often boats were pulled along on ropes by men and oxen who walked along the riverbank.

Large ships were built in special shipyards and were used for long sea voyages. These ships were longer and much narrower than rowboats. They also had sails.

Goods were transported in Sumer by using sledges, wagons, chariots, and boats. **Merchants** from Sumer led caravans carrying barley and textiles to Asia Minor and Iran.

The ports of major cities were busy places. Ships called "galleys" were used for trade. They carried timber, metals, and other items across the Arabian Sea.

Sumerian trade routes were extensive.

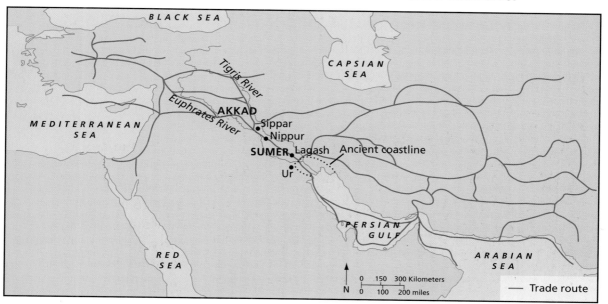

Weapons and Warfare

The rulers of the different Sumerian **city-states** were always fighting each other for control of the region. They fought over who had a right to use the land and water. They also fought for power.

Armies

A specialized class of warriors developed around 3000 B.C.E. When a war arose between neighboring city-states, the king was responsible for stopping it. Each king had a regular army. These were soldiers who were trained to fight battles—this was their job. The major weapon used in attacking was the chariot. It could be driven into a group of soldiers. It was slow, but faster than soldiers on foot. Following the chariots was the infantry, wearing armor and carrying weapons. The soldiers attacked in a **phalanx** formation. In a phalanx formation, the men

This picture shows a battering ram used in battle to break through a wall or gate. Behind it are archers with bows and arrows.

This picture shows men carrying lances and long shields. Their shields are close together in a phalanx formation.

march so close together that their shields overlap.

The Sumerians won many battles against armies of other kings trying to gain control of their land. The Sumerians had superior weapons, military tactics, and leadership.

Weapons

Some of the weapons Sumerians used in battle included iron-headed battering rams and other siege weapons, perhaps a catapult.

Weapons such as lances and arrows were made of wood. The lance points, arrowheads, swords, daggers, and harpoons were often made of copper and bronze.

Height of the Sumerian Civilization

Writing

Sumerians began to write down their words around 2500 B.C.E. They wrote many long poems about the heroic deeds of their gods. There were poems and legends about kings.

Chariots made travel easier and gave Sumerians an advantage in warfare.

Religion

The religion of the Sumerians is the oldest recorded religion. As Sumer was conquered at different times by other countries such as Babylonia and Assyria, their religion remained basically the same.

Laws

The Sumerians developed a set of laws, or codes, and wrote them on clay **tablets.** Ur-Nammu became King of Ur in about 2100 B.C.E. Ur-Nammu is also known for his law code. It was written 300 years before the Code of Hammurabi of Babylon. Systems of law in other areas seem to be patterned after the law codes of Sumer.

The Sumerians built the first wheeled vehicle. Here is a model of an early Sumerian chariot.

Inventions

The Sumerians increased the knowledge of mathematics by developing the **sexagesimal** system based on the number 60. In order to make trade easier, they worked out a system of uniform weights and measures. The

This Sumerian wheel is made of wood and held together with bands. The wheel made it easier to take goods to other parts of the area.

Sumerians invented the potters wheel, the wheeled vehicle, and the sailboat. These inventions helped to make the manufacturing of goods easier.

Travel

Sumerian teachers and **scribes** traveled to other lands. They seem to have influenced many areas of religion and literature in the Near East.

Art

The major art of Sumer was architecture. Sumerians built **temples** with stone foundations and platforms. These temples had painted walls and alters. They had mosaic columns and facades. The Sumerians also made beautiful works of art from gold, silver, and copper. They carved many figurines as well as statues of their kings.

Semitic Rule

Semite nomads came from Syria in about 4000 B.C.E. They settled along the Euphrates River to the north of Sumer. This land was known as Akkad.

Sargon

One of the most famous Semites was a leader named Sargon the Great. He was born around 2350 B.C.E. He was a military leader and king. He left many records of his conquests. Sargon managed to bring Sumer and the northern half of Mesopotamia into one nation with one king. His empire lasted nearly 200 years.

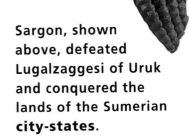

Sargon, shown above, defeated Lugalzaggesi of Uruk and conquered the lands of the Sumerian **city-states**.

Sargon built the port city of Agade. Ships from as far off as India, Egypt, and Ethiopia docked at the ports. Agade became prosperous from trade. Most of the citizens of Agade were Semites. The language spoken by the Semites was known as Akkadian.

The Gutians

By 2200 B.C.E., the city of Agade was invaded and destroyed by warriors called Gutians from the mountains to the northeast. The city was so completely destroyed that its ruins have not yet been found. The Gutians founded a dynasty that included all of Sumer and Akkad.

By 2100 B.C.E. the Sumerian city of Ur became powerful again, but the power of Sumer did not last long. In 2000 B.C.E. the Elamites, from Elam, to the east of Sumer, attacked and destroyed Ur.

Hammurabi

Finally, a Semitic ruler named Hammurabi came to power in the region. He attacked and defeated the kings of the surrounding cities. In 1750 B.C.E. Hammurabi was ruler of the Babylonian Empire. His empire reached from the Persian Gulf to the Habur River. This brought about the end of Sumer.

This is a Babylonian map of the world. It shows the extent of their empire.

Decline of the Sumerian Civilization

Constant fighting

The Sumerians were constantly at war with other countries as well as with each other. This continual fighting led to their eventual downfall. Many times, the powerful **city-states** of Sumer were conquered and destroyed, only to be rebuilt.

Around 2000 B.C.E., the city of Ur was destroyed by the Elamites and the king of Ur was taken captive. After this, the power of Sumer faded, but the culture remained.

Babylonia extended well beyond the Sumerian empire.

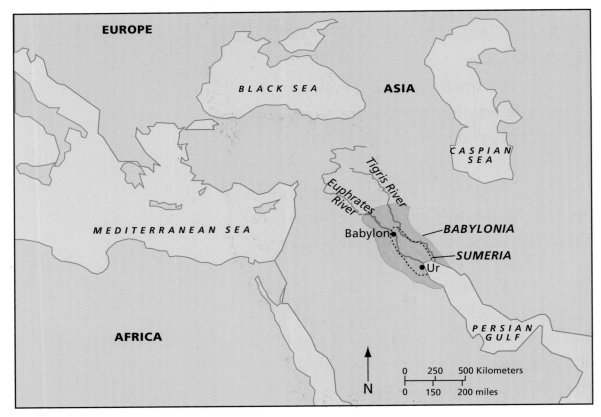

The Ishtar Gate was built by the Babylonians. Its size and complexity indicates the architectural achievements of the Babylonians.

The Babylonians

In 1850 B.C.E., the Babylonians conquered Sumer. The art, literature, schools, religion, and mythology of the Babylonians was almost the same as that of the Sumerians. The region that was Sumer became part of the Babylonian empire, and the Sumerians were soon considered to be Babylonians.

As the Babylonians traveled, they carried the Sumerian system of laws, learning, and business methods to other countries. The only difference between the Sumerians and Babylonians was their language.

Time Line

4000–3500 B.C.E. The first Sumerians settled on the banks of the Euphrates River. It is possible they came from central Asia.

The first know vehicle with wooden wheels was built by the Sumerians.

A **temple** was built at Eridu. This was an early example of the **ziggurat.**

Settlements began to change into **city-states.**

The potters wheel began to be used.

3200 B.C.E. The White Temple was built and dedicated to An, the Sumerian sun god.

3100 B.C.E. Sumerians began writing on clay **tablets.**

3000 B.C.E. Democratic assemblies changed to kingships.

Etanna of Kish became the first ruler of Sumer.

Colored mosaics were used as decoration for buildings.

Kish became the leading city of Sumer.

Meskiaggasher became king of Uruk.

Hundreds of clay tablets with writing on them were discovered at Uruk from this time period.

The plano-convex brick was introduced.

2800 B.C.E. Ur became a city-state.

2750 B.C.E. The first formal contracts for land sales were drawn up in **cuneiform** writing.

Small, simple palaces were built at the Sumerian cities of Eridu and Kish.

"Praying statues" were found at Tell Asmar from this time period. These statues were placed in the temple to offer continual prayer for an individual.

The "Standard of Ur" was buried in a tomb at Ur. Buried with it were many statues and gold and silver **artifacts.**

2700 B.C.E. Gilgamesh became king of Uruk.

2500 B.C.E. The Sumerians began making glass.

Tablets were discovered from this time period that show contracts, land sales, and lists of names.

2425 B.C.E. The **Stele** of King Eannatum was made. It shows the king and his army in battle on one side, and on the other side, the god Ningirsu holding the defeated army in a net.

2350 B.C.E. Sargon the Great was born.

2300 B.C.E. The city of Agade was built by Sargon the Great.

2200 B.C.E. Sumer was captured by the Gutians.

The city of Agade was destroyed.

Prince Gudea was ruler of Lagash even though the Gutians were in control of the region.

2150 B.C.E. Utehegal of Uruk, who became King of Sumer, overthrew the Gutians.

2100 B.C.E. Ur-Nammu built a ziggurat at Ur and dedicated it to the moon god, Nanna.

Ur-Nammu wrote a code of laws.

2100–2004 B.C.E. The Dynasty of Ur was founded by Ur-Nammu.

2000 B.C.E. The Elamites attacked and destroyed the city of Ur.

1850 B.C.E. Sumer was conquered by the Babylonians.

Glossary

ad hoc gathered for a specific purpose

archaeology study of the graves, tools, and pottery from past human life and culture

artifact object made by people

artisan skilled craftworker

bas-relief sculpture in which the important detail is raised from the background

bazaar street lined with shops and stalls, often found in the Middle East

city-state politically independent city

cuneiform form of early writing that uses wedge-shaped characters

deity god or goddess

epigraphy study of ancient inscriptions. One who studies these inscriptions is called an epigraphist.

excavate to carefully dig up buried objects to find information about the past

filigree delicate openwork of fine wire such as silver or gold. It is often used in jewelry.

hearth brick or stone floor of a fireplace that usually extends into the room

inscribe to cut letters, numbers, or patterns into a solid surface

irrigate to water crops by channeling water from a river or lake along pipes or ditches

lapidary person who cuts, polishes, or engraves gems

lapis lazuli semi-precious, deep blue stone

levee ridge that prevents flooding

lyre stringed instrument belonging to the harp family

magazine storehouse for goods and ammunition

merchant person who buys goods in one place and sells them in another, often a different country

mortar dish in which a substance can be crushed with a pestle

netherworld world of the dead

offering something given as a part of worship

pestle club shaped tool for grinding something in a mortar

phalanx line of soldiers carrying overlapping shields and long swords

porridge soft food made by boiling oatmeal or other meal in water or milk

poultice soft medicine spread on a pad and applied to wounds

reservoir artificial lake

scribe person who writes for a living; they usually had to go to a special school to learn

script system of writing

sexagesimal numerical system based on the number 60

shrine place where a person goes to worship a particular god or goddess; the room usually contains a religious image

sledge vehicle on low runners, pulled by oxen or horses. It is usually used to carry heavy loads.

stele upright stone with an inscribed or sculptured surface. It is used for commemorative purposes.

tablet flat piece of clay or stone with words or pictures on it

temple place where people worship their gods and goddesses

whitewash mixture of lime, water, and white color; used to paint walls and fences

whorl small wheel that regulates the speed of a spinning wheel

ziggurat temple tower built as a terraced pyramid

More Books to Read

Anness Publishing Staff. *Ancient Civilizations.* New York: Anness Publishing, Inc., 1999.

Martell, Hazel Mary. *The Kingfisher Book of Ancient Civilizations.* Portland, Ore.: Kingfisher, 2001.

Sasson, Jack (ed.). *Civilizations of the Ancient Near East.* Peabody, Mass.: Hendrickson Publishers, Inc., 2000.

Index